Copyright © Palak Tewary, 2024

The author asserts the moral right under the Copyright, Designs and Patents Act 1988 to be identified as the author of this work

All Right Reserved. No part of this publication may be reproduced, stored in a retrieval system or transmitted, in any form or by any means without the prior consent of the author, nor be otherwise circulated in any form of binding or cover other than that which it is published, with the exception of certain activities permitted by applicable copyright laws, such as brief quotations in the context of a review or academic work

Publisher: Powerful Thoughts

Dedication

To Ma, Pa & Princess
for always believing in me

Contents

A Promise to Myself 11
A Quest for the Truth 12
A Season of both Night and Day 13
A Simple Walk...in times of Covid 14
Can't 15
Conflicts 16
Danube Island 17
Dark Clouds 18
Different yet the Same 19
Dolphin 20
Earth's Warning 21
Every Woman's Song 22
From a Portrait's View 23
Heartbreak 24
I carry you within me 25
I shall miss, when lockdown ends 26
In Shadows Cast 27
Just be 28
Labyrinth of Existence 29
Letting go of Regrets 30
No Country of my own 31

Oh, my dear world	32
Rain	33
Recipe for world war	34
Refuge within	35
State of Struggle	36
Stood Up	37
Strange Visitor	38
The Beauty of the Human Mind	39
The Pursuit of Tranquillity	40
This, too, shall pass…	42
Through Simba's eyes	43
Time for me…amid Pandemic	44
Time gone by…	46
Winter Magic	47
World	48
Different forms of poetry explained	49
Blank Verse Poem	50
Couplets	51
Dodoitsu Poem	52
Free Verse Poem	53
Haiku Poem	54
Kennings Poem	55
Landay Poem	56

Magic 9 Poem 57
Pathya Vat Poem 58
Prose Poem 59
Rhyming Poetry 60
Shape Poetry 61
Terza Rima Poem 62
Trecet Poem 63
Triolet Poem 64
Villanella Poem 65
Guess the poetry form 67
The Poems and their forms 71
About the Author 75

A Promise to Myself

(First published on pentoprint.org)
...inspired by a wish for a better tomorrow

As the first of the new year bells
I stand resolute in my good intentions
And with excitement my heart swells
Telling me that this year shall be different
Oh! I shall do as my eager mind compels
And not let boredom or weariness set in
To bid all my noble plans farewells
If I can hold a month onto these pretensions
Perchance my promises shan't be empty shells

A Quest for the Truth
...inspired by a wish for seeking verity

The change of the winds,
the silence before the storm
the small signs that were not the norm

An unaware mind and a sleeping intuition,
but now an unfulfilling pursuit of the truth
through a nightmare – the only unimaginable route

A Season of both Night and Day

(First published on pentoprint.org)
...inspired by a wish for equilibrium

It's spring; differences at play
Flowers bloom and rain falls
A season of both night and day

Strong winds and skies are grey
Yet sunshine thaws the walls
It's spring; differences at play

Cool air, but hearts are gay
Nature answers the warming calls
A season of both night and day

Fresh buds in its array
Amid melting icy squalls
It's spring; differences at play

Singing birds flying away
To answer nature's calls
A season of both night and day

World awakening from its stay
In winter's cold dark halls
It's spring; differences at play
A season of both night and day

A Simple Walk...in times of Covid
...inspired by a wish for normalcy

Cheerful nods and smiles
exchanged during ambling walks
in the local park
….no news!

Fearful eyes, masked face,
crossing pavements during
hurried, worried walks
…strange indeed!

Can't....
...inspired by a wish for breakthrough

Engulfed in darkness,
I can't see……but a faint glimmer of light
Way beyond!

Torn in sorrow,
I can't hear……but the hollow echoes calling
Far across!

Afraid in the mist,
I can't hold……but the cold air swirling
Just around!

Unaided in the world,
I can't smile……but at life laughing
So hard!

Conflicts

(First published on pentoprint.org)

...inspired by a wish for resurgence

doves up in the sky	white silk their furs
content and peaceful	beguiling the world
peacocks in the parks	showing off their feathers
delighted and happy	charming the world
sea in its glory	throwing huge waves
beautiful and glorious	delighting the world
sky up above	perfect in every way
clear and sunny	enchanting the world
me in my melancholy	locked in a cage
flustered and fighting	defying the world

Danube Island

(First appeared on worldjam.co.uk)
...inspired by a wish for travel

You, who captured my heart, are
miles afar and too far out of reach.
The sandy dunes on the desolate beach,
where a piece of heaven resides.

There lives a magic in you
that can turn, even the tides.
Closing my eyes, I feel your glides,
oh, crystal river, I wish you were near.

Dark Clouds
(First published on pentoprint.org)
...inspired by a wish for unburdening

Wisps of grey fluff
miserably running in the
sky, making waves in their own fashion,
trying to escape from themselves,
enveloping the mountains in their dark
velvety folds,
hanging low as if awaiting an invitation
to pour out all their grief
and then, finally, lazily breathing
out blue and cool smoke

Different yet the Same
(First published on pentoprint.org)
...inspired by a wish for harmony in diversity

Someone's misery, someone's joy
Both – by the very same ploy

Each eye – a diverse vision
Every day – another tension
Each word – a different position
Every way – a separate direction

Difference in how we live
Contrast in what we believe
Dispute in everything we hear
Change is the one thing we fear

BUT

Sometimes blue, sometimes green
Sometimes both – the sea is seen

Each heart – a similar beat
Each sun - the equal heat
Each hour – the constant minutes
Each being – compeer spirits

Empathy in how we heal
Compassion in what we feel
Kindness in everything we say
Humanity is the one thing to display

Dolphin
...inspired by a wish to swim the seas

Water-dweller
Aqua-mammal
Ocean-jumper
Social-animal
Speed-traveller
Beauty-example

Earth's Warning

(First published on pentoprint.org)

...inspired by a wish for beauty in nature

       from the fields of gilded corn and blushed wheat
to the pathways covered with yellow and amber leaves
       the autumn bloom spreads its wings
       and a magical hue, the wind weaves

the clouds cast their tormenting net in the open air
       and a rainy spell could destroy us whole
a pitch-dark blackness that overwhelms
       and a brutalising fear, in the middle of the soul

       but then the morning rays of the golden sun
gently touch the rolling hills bursting with crops
       the stream smoothly bubbles along
keeping pace as the chestnut horse gallops

       yes, a fickle mistress, the land lures
bestowing treasures, as it bids - although
do remember: the humble lesson harvests teach
       we can only reap as we sow

Every Woman's Song
...inspired by a wish for flying without fear

In the whispers of the morning light,
Where dreams and shadows softly meet,
There lies a tale of strength and grace,
In every woman, ever sweet

She's the melody in life's refrain,
The gentle breeze that guides the way,
With courage woven in her soul,
She faces each and every day

In her eyes, the stars dance free,
Reflecting galaxies unseen,
Her spirit, boundless as the sea,
Her presence, like a tranquil stream

She walks with dignity and pride,
Her laughter echoes through the air,
A symphony of joy and love,
A testament to all she bears

She carries burdens, yet she soars,
With wings of hope and resilience,
In her heart, a fire ignites,
Fuelled by dreams and perseverance

She's the keeper of stories untold,
The guardian of wisdom's light,
With hands that heal and hearts that mend,
She paints the world with colours bright

So, here's to every woman's song,
A tune of strength and grace,
In her, the universe finds its voice,
A timeless beauty, an eternal embrace

From a Portrait's View
...inspired by a wish for real connections

A hurried affair, early morning was;
No time to speak, no time to hear
They all rushed out one by one,
Till there was no one near

The evening brought back life into the home,
The boredom of the day, eradicated
Low voiced murmurs then each split to their own domain
Until the evening meal was presented

Each on their phone, typing away, & watching the tv,
Until the neighbour came to call
Then they were all laughing together, exchanging banter
Silence reigned again, once she was over the wall

They never watched me, watching them,
Unblinking, adjudging, wide-eyed
If they had known that I could see,
Would they have behaved the same or just lied?

Heartbreak
...inspired by a wish for trusting destiny

The mind, no thought and the heart, no song
Living in impassive void where the soul doesn't belong

The role, no grit and the will, no fire
Living in cold apathy where the part doesn't inspire

The style, no mark and the brand, no worth
Living in derision where the treasure doesn't unearth

The dream, no truth and the wish, no feel
Living in detached abyss where the spirit doesn't heal

The clock, no stop and the life, no break
Living in a shifting world, in time, the heart doesn't ache

I carry you within me
(First published on pentoprint.org)
...inspired by a wish for belonging

It's not a place for me
It's not a sight that I see
It's not the possessions that I possess
And it's most definitely not an address

It's not a smell that I smell
It's not a word that I spell
It's not the sounds that I hear
And it's most definitely not how I appear

It is buried deep inside
It is always along for the ride
It is what sets me free
Home is what I carry within me

I shall miss, when lockdown ends

(First published on pentoprint.org)

...inspired by a wish for simple pleasures

The lazy routine of the mornings
Taking a moment to savour the smell of the new coffee blends
Sitting in the sunshine or watching as the bird sings
The jaunty chatter of the family, the cheery giggling with friends

The happiness that I found within, not without
The little notes to myself that I now penned
Alas, the joy of just being, just living, devout
The luxury of time that I now have, to spend

Those video calls that we make every week
Sitting up late because we just had to watch another episode
The fun and games and dressing up half-chic
This uncharted spell...where everything seemed to have slowed

The release of my creative spirit in new and unfound ways
Doing things that I have, perhaps, forgotten in life's contends
Little keepsakes made and added to my treasured arrays
I shall miss, when lockdown ends

In Shadows Cast
...inspired by a wish for accepting myself

In shadows cast, I find my face,
A spectral of shades, I see,
Embracing every hue and trace.

In dusky depths, I find my place,
Where light and darkness intertwine,
In shadows cast, I find my face.

I dance with shadows, interlace
The fragments of my soul's design,
Embracing every hue and trace.

Through twilight's veil, I boldly chase
The mysteries that lie beneath,
In shadows cast, I find my face.

With every step, I boldly embrace
The varied tones that make me whole,
Embracing every hue and trace.

So let the shadows now efface
The boundaries of what I can be,
In shadows cast, I find my face,
Embracing every hue and trace.

Just be
...inspired by a wish for smelling the roses

In hectic days, I seek a slower pace
A quiet hour, a moment's gentle rest
To find a calm, a consecrated space

Amid the rush, I yearn to feel more blessed
To breathe in deep, and let the chaos cease
And drop the weights heavy on my chest

In serenity found, a simple, silent peace
The world slows down, and time itself rewinds
In mindful moments, all my qualms decrease

Within this quiet, new freshness unwinds
A chance to savour life, to truly see
The beauty in the now, what delight it finds

So, I will pause, clasp this gentle plea
To take my time, and let my spirit be

Labyrinth of Existence
(First published on pentoprint.org)
<u>*...inspired by a wish for untangling the mess*</u>

```
We
  are
   all
    connected
       by the
          intricate
             design
                of
                 the
                  web
                   called
                      life.   No
                   connected        matter
                      we are all      where
                          where         we |
                          world         are –
                          elementary    thickly
                          this          spun
                          most of       in
                          make          this
                          they          three
                          and yet       dimensional
                          our beats,    world –
                          our souls,    we
                          our feelings, are all
                          our thoughts, connected.
                          to see –   Illuminated
                          unable     within –
                          are        there
                          we         are
                              matters
```

Letting go of Regrets
(First published on pentoprint.org)
...inspired by a wish for clarity of thought

Cuddled up on the window seat,
one lazy sunny beautiful afternoon,
with me, I am determined to meet.

The pale sunray falls into the saloon,
and lights up the shadowed places,
and fills it with a delightful sweet tune.

The wind caresses the lost spaces,
letting the air breathe and hum with
songs of forgotten stories and faces.

I decode my own magic and myth,
revisiting the pathways that I chose,
unlocking doors without the locksmith.

Absolving myself, many a chapters I close,
albeit with thorns I may be, but I am a rose.

No Country of my own
...inspired by a wish for homecoming

But in the depths of solitude, I find,
A strength in roots that intertwine.
Though scattered far, they hold me tight,
Binding me to the world's delight.

For my country is not in soil or stone,
But in the love and kinship I've known.
In every smile, in every face,
I find my home, my sacred space.

So let the winds of fate blow strong,
I'll journey forth, where I belong.
For though I roam with no country of my own,
My heart, my soul, will always be homegrown

Oh, my dear world
(First published on palaktewary.com)
...inspired by a wish for peace

Oh, my dear world, I hear your cry...
For the loss of humanity and all the pain and suffering...
One voice that I am, how do I try...
To eliminate the bias, the hate and the hate-mongering...

Oh, my dear world, I hear you shout...
The message of love and peace...
One voice that I am, what's my clout...
To ask when will this violence cease...

Oh, my dear world, I hear you say...
That the finger pointing only leads to more conflict...
One voice that I am, how do I keep at bay...
Stones from being hurled and even mere words to not prick...

Oh, my dear world, I hear you ask....
If not you, then who...
Though one voice that I am, I join this task...
My fellow beings it's not just for me & you...

For our world, our generations, our humanity...
Let's try and stop this insanity...

Rain

(First published on pentoprint.org)
...inspired by a wish for finding joy in all

As I sit by my window sill,
the rain drops start to patter,
I feel a smile find its way to my lips,
and all the worries no longer matter.

As I hold out my hand to stop their race,
the rain drops start to spatter,
I feel a wetness find its way to my face,
and of tears and beams, I get the latter.

As I step outside and feel the water,
the rain drops start to scatter
I feel a twitch find its way to my legs,
and my feet start to clatter.

As I dance around and sing in the rain,
the rain drops start to natter,
I feel a joy find its way to my heart, and
my delusion about sunshine starts to shatter.

Recipe for world war
...inspired by a wish for non-violence

Take a country filled with greed to expand
Add in a few thousand ardent proponents
Whisk ½ kilo of another nation's wish to protect its land
Place a pinch of yet another's fight for dignity
Sprinkle 2 tubs of a few realms' ulterior motives
Mix in betrayal, misdirection and misinformation
Stir in numerous arms and explosives
And squeeze in frenzied ardour for power
Grease with dwindling economies galore
Fork the mixture and bake at 100^0C
Serve a perfectly hardened world war
Garnish with pain and suffering

Refuge within
...inspired by a wish for controlling my mind

In the whirlwind of life's endless race,
I find myself lost in the crowded fray,
Each passing moment a frantic chase,
In the whirlwind of life's endless race.
Overwhelmed by the frenetic pace,
I yearn for peace to come my way,
In the whirlwind of life's endless race,
I find myself lost in the crowded fray.

Every task a mountain to embrace,
As deadlines loom and pressures weigh,
Caught in a cycle I can't efface,
Every task a mountain to embrace.
Yet amid the chaos, I seek solace,
A moment of respite, come what may,
Every task a mountain to embrace,
As deadlines loom and pressures weigh.

But in the stillness, I find my grace,
A quiet refuge where worries sway,
Where burdens lift and troubles erase,
In the stillness, I find my grace.
No longer lost in the frantic pace,
I breathe in calmness, day by day,
In the stillness, I find my grace,
A quiet refuge where worries sway.

State of Struggle
...inspired by a wish for liberation

Torn in worry, the nightmare beckons
Stepping into it, seems the only farcical way

Chains of doubt, binding all the dreams tight
Through the storm, I explore for dawn's opening of day

And hope's whisper, ignites a fierce fight
A candle in the tempest, glows bright its modest ray

Through fire and fear, footsteps on the path
With whispered prayers, I shall outlast the wrath that lay

Stood Up
...inspired by a wish for confidence

Michelin-star restaurant,
scrumptious meal, a view to die-
for and I, in my best frock –
looking at the clock.

Strange Visitor

(First published on Fly on the Wall Poetry)
...inspired by a wish for camaraderie

Stranger
in our midst.
Ask it – yes do.
What does it want?
Is it an enemy or a friend or just an unknown stranger
that has lost its way and is now as terrified of us
as we are of it? We call him an alien. What does it call
us? Can you not ask?
Do ask - yes do.
If it tells us it's from another place – will we believe?
We will - just coz it has one eye and two mouths.
And then we will alienise it just as we do those –
which are
different   race   colour
gender   religion   orientation
or simply   just different   than you,
so why   should   this
outsider not be considered so utterly outlandish? -
even though it may be more terrified that we are.

The Beauty of the Human Mind

(First published on pentoprint.org)

...inspired by a wish for believing in the journey

In springtime's dawn, oppositions reign,
As ice and warmth, sun and rain,
Collide in nature's grand display,
A dance of contraries in play.

The thaw starts, the ice gives way,
As winter's clutch begins to sway,
And yet, the chill still lingers on,
An enigma, oh, so strong.

The earth awakens, buds appear,
A time of growth, a time of cheer,
And yet, the storms they do not cease,
A puzzle, oh, inner peace.

The spring's conflicts do persist,
A paradox of sorts, that we can't resist,
For life is made of opposites,
Of joy and ache, of likes and dislikes.

So let us embrace the birth of spring,
With all the challenges it brings,
For in the paradox we find,
The beauty of the human mind.

The Pursuit of Tranquillity
...inspired by a wish for contentment

In search of peace, I roam the world's expanse,
Seeking contentment in each distant land,
Yet find it eludes me, a fleeting wisp,
Like shadows chased by the relentless sun.
Through valleys deep and mountains towering high,
I search for solace, unaware it lies.

In bustling streets where chaos never lies,
I seek a haven, a tranquil expanse,
But peace evades me, as the days pass by,
A distant dream in a far-off land,
An oasis shimmering 'neath the sun,
Its mirage fades, a vanishing wisp.

Through trials and triumphs, I grasp at each wisp,
Yearning for the serenity that lies
Beyond the reach of the relentless sun,
Yet in my heart, I sense a quiet expanse,
A boundless landscape, an inner land,
Where true contentment waits, never to fly.

With open eyes, I cease to chase and fly,
No longer grasping at the elusive wisp,
For within myself, I find the land
Where joy and peace eternally lie,
An endless expanse, a boundless land,
Unveiled beneath the radiant sun.

In silent moments, beneath the sun,
I feel the warmth of peace begin to fly,
A gentle breeze across the tranquil land,
No longer just a fleeting wisp,
But a steadfast presence where truth does lie,
In the depths of my own inner expanse.

So let the sun illuminate the expanse,
As I release the need to chase and fly,
For in my soul, true contentment does lie,
No longer just a fleeting wisp,
But a boundless land beneath the sun,
Within myself, where peace will always land.

This, too, shall pass...
(First published on pentoprint.org)
...inspired by a wish for strength

Changed times, changed situations
Changed people, changed emotions
It is all but a play of destiny
Bleak at times, and at times – shiny

Some rise when stumble, some – fall
Some are beaten by time, some – not at all
Its the test of time that tells
On which side someone dwells

Wanting to change things, but can not
When frustration and darkness seem to be your lot
It's the strength within, that can show a light
On finding peace despite your plight

There are moments in time, when all hopes fade
And then there are moments, when one just smiles at fate
Time – silences, comforts, tires and heals
Time – moves on – a constant never-ending wheel

Through Simba's eyes
...inspired by a wish for perspective

Humid. Arid afternoon. Lazy. The Pride watches. As another one comes by, along the rugged landscape. Anxious to find space within the fast-forming circle. Around us. Amidst tall blades of grass. They sit, watchful

and silent. In cages. Made of steel and aluminium. That purr like cats. I lick mother's face. She nudges head at me. Cameras' click. Smiles. Rafiki runs past. Run behind. Play. Jump. Shouts and screams. Screams

and shouts. Smiles. Cameras' click. Puzzled. Turn to look. Fingers point at me. Scared. Run to father. Cling on mane. A piercing screech of tire. One comes closer. And closer. And closer. Mother nudges head at me.

It's safari. They just want to see.

Time for me...amid Pandemic
...inspired by a wish for evolving

7am - An unnerving silence filled the air, there was no rush nor agenda today I could laze in, take a while to get out of bed – I lay there and wondered what to do in the hours that stretched out before me...like a pristine page of an old diary that has been unused and now suddenly, you must fill it up. I looked at the clock – only four minutes had passed since I woke. Turning to social media - full of stories of the pandemic, lockdown and numbers.... So many numbers – the cases, the countries, the deaths.... It was agonising, yet strangely absorbing that I couldn't put away the devices.

Mid-morning – I had dressed, cooked, cleaned and been for the walk that was allowed – the one hour of fresh air, which I duly took. After all, must take care of our health. Averting paths to avoid everyone. Made a call and then another and then another – oh! this was fun. Perhaps, staying home won't be so bad. But after the fourth repetition of the same things – I went to bed for a nap. Ahh...was that a crack in the ceiling....no just a shadow. A rumbling stomach took me off to lunch...I set the table – I shouldn't behave like a beast and eat over the sink...even though there is no one to see.

Afternoon – I signed up for three different OTT platforms...really, everyone is signing up so why not me. But then, before pressing the final place order button, I stopped. I reviewed the total that it would cost – I bit my lip, maybe three was OTT. I purchased one and closed the browsers for the other two. Maybe once things improved – I sighed, there is always hope. Like a child, with a new toy – afternoon turned to evening and then to night as I watched a movie after another and started off on a series – ten seasons long. Surely that would keep me busy till next week. Happy to escape – I entered the world of the make-believe.

3 days later – am done with the series as my nights have turned to days and I have mislaid all sense of time. Oh – the one-hour walk is still there – how can it not be? Must take care of the health – but it now happens with an earphone stuck to my ear to catch up on the few calls that still remain as I don't want to miss watching the unreal world. The series – ah yes, a sense of desolation creeps up – like I have lost touch with my best friends. I must find another one soon. There are so many – I make a list to binge watch. Now, I won't have to do without. I have a list. I have a list, my heart sings.

3 weeks later – I lay listless on the bed. I have given up on news days ago and the one or two calls that remain are easily dealt with and don't require much effort. Tired of cooking, it's now cereal and bread and chocolate and coffee. A fatigue – that is, perhaps, more of the soul rather than the body, has gripped me. I cannot move – I do not want to move. Nothing could entice me to move – not the real world nor the unreal one. Until the phone pings and an alert pops up – World Meditation Day – 21st May. A tiny flicker of interest burns deep inside. An idea– that perhaps, I must take care of my mind first before I take care of my health.

3 months later – I chirpily wake up, practice meditation and yoga, head off for my walk. Yes, back to moving now. I have baked a delicious pie and am ready for my series of webinars planned for the day. But before that, I make the video calls to family and friends. Oh wait, I forgot my lipstick. There, that's better. I have learnt – how to utilise this gift of time - I paint, I sing, I dance, I read and I write. I drive to the local park and sit by the water just being one with the nature. I laugh, I smile, I find joy in the smallest of things and yes, I do watch a series – one episode only - daily. I have found the sense of time – time for me.

Time gone by...
...inspired by a wish for progression

Que sera sera......
with this thought in my mind
with this motto in my head
I pass my days
in a faint hope
of days gone by
of time slipped away
returning just once more

Que sera sera......
with this dream in my heart
with this wish in my soul
I slowly let go
of the faint hope
of time that didn't move
of days that weren't empty
pinning my gaze on the year next

Winter Magic

(First published on pentoprint.org)

...inspired by a wish for making dreams flourish

Eggnogs by the cheery fire
as the mellifluous snow falls
lighting up a hidden desire
to dream a new dream
that shall even inspire
the untamed snowmen
to brazenly boldly conspire
with all the mountain walls
to scale the skies higher

World

(First published on Anthology – A Passion for Poetry, 2002)

...inspired by a wish for kindness

Like frogs in the well,
Unaware of the sea,
We live our lives- separately,
Your world and mine.

We see but we don't look,
We hear but we don't listen,
We talk but we don't understand,
Your world and mine.

But when the suns sets,
The birds return home,
And the night falls...it feels like one..
Your world and mine!

Different forms of poetry explained

Poetry conveys a thought, a story, an idea in a lyrical arrangement of words. There are many ways to structure poems with lines and meters and syllables and beats and stanzas. It can also be freeform with no structure. These are just a few types of forms explained, which are used in this poetry book.

Blank Verse Poem

Blank Verse Poems are poems with a precise meter called iambic pentameter – but that does not rhyme.

This means that each line contains five iambs – two syllable pairs where the second syllable is more pronounced / emphasized.

Couplets

A couplet is made up of two consecutive poetry lines that create an idea or thought.

These have similar syllabic pattern called a meter. Most couplets tend to rhyme, but not all do.

These can be within a larger poem or be a poem on its own.

Dodoitsu Poem

This is a Japanese poetic form and does not have meter or rhyme constraints but focuses on syllables instead.

The key points of this poetry form is:

- It is a 4-line poem
- The first 3 lines have 7 syllables each
- The fourth line and final line has 5 syllables each
- The focus of the poem is usually on love or work with a comical twist

Free Verse Poem

Free verse poems tend to lack a consistent pattern, scheme, rhyme, metre or musical form.

They are not devoid of structure but there is a lot of leeway allowed when composing a free verse poem, especially when compared to other poetry forms which are stricter such as black verse.

Haiku Poem

A Japanese poetry form, Haiku, is made of short unrhymed lines that conjure natural imagery.

It can come in various formats of short verses but the most common is a three-line poem with a syllable pattern of five-seven-five.

Kennings Poem

A kenning is a two-word phrase describing an object, often using a metaphor.

A kennings poem is a made up of several lines of kennings to describe something or someone. It can be made up of any number of kennings.

Landay Poem

The landay originates from nomads of Afghanistan, India etc. It is based off a couplet and can be of variable length – as concise as two lines or run on for several pages.

The basic rules are:

- It can be comprised of self-contained couplets
- There are 9 syllables in first line & 13 syllables in second line
- These usually focus on saying the harsh truth using wit – themes can be of love, grief, war, separation, homeland etc.

Magic 9 Poem

This is a new form and seems to be ...inspired by a poet misspelling the word "abracadabra"

It is a 9-line poem with no rules relating to meter or subject matter – but it follows as rhyme scheme - abacadaba

Pathya Vat Poem

This is a Cambodian verse form. It has 4 lines of 4 syllables each where lines 2 and 3 rhyme.

If the poem has more than one stanza then the last line of previous stanza rhymes with second and third lines of the following one.

Prose Poem

Prose poetry combines elements of lyrical and metre of a traditional poetry along with language of prose like punctuation, lack of line breaks etc.

There is no fixed definition of prose poetry however it may include elements such as:

- repetition
- resonance
- a metrical or rhythmic structure
- soft or hard rhymes
- metaphors
- figures of speeches

etc.

Rhyming Poetry

This sort of poetry forms a rhyme scheme that repeats at the end of a line or stanza. The schemes can change line by line, stanza by stanza, or can continue throughout a poem.

Poems with rhyme schemes are generally written in formal verse, which has a strict meter: a repeating pattern of stressed and unstressed syllables.

The design is fixed by letters of the alphabet. Lines elected with the same letter rhyme with each other. For example, the rhyme scheme ABAB means the first and third lines of a stanza, or the "A"s, rhyme with each other, and the second line rhymes with the fourth line, or the "B"s rhyme together.

There are various types of schemes such as:

- Alternate rhyme - ABAB
- Ballade – ABABBCBC
- Coupled rhyme - AABB
- Enclosed rhyme – ABBA
- Simple four-line rhyme – ABCB

Etc.

The beauty about this type of poetry is that you can have any type of scheme you like.

Shape Poetry

In this poetry form, the poem takes on a shape of its subject.

Therefore, the arrangement of the words on paper will reflect the shape of the subject matter of the poem. It is more a visual form of poetry.

Terza Rima Poem

A rhyming verse form, consisting of:

- tercets (three-line stanzas)
- with an interlocking three-line rhyme scheme where last word of second line in one tercet provides rhyme for the first and third lines in tercet that follows i.e., aba bcb cdc ded ee
- The poem ends with either a single line or a couplet that rhymes with previous tercets's middle line.

Trecet Poem

This poem has 3 lines of poetry forming a stanza or a poem.

There are no set rhyme schemes or meters.

It is usually a slower-paced poem allowing readers to focus on subject matter.

The length of each line can be varied

Triolet Poem

These are stanzas of 8-lines poem where the first line is used 3 times and the second line is used twice and it has a rhyme scheme of the other lines with the first and second line as follows:

- A (first line)
- B (second line)
- a (rhymes with first line)
- A (repeat first line)
- a (rhymes with first line)
- b (rhymes with second line)
- A (repeat first line)
- B (repeat second line)

Villanella Poem

This is a poetic form that has 19 lines and uses repeated lines and a strict rhyming pattern.

There is a lyrical quality to this type of poem with their structured lines.

A type of poem with:
- total of six stanzas
- five three-line stanzas that follow a rhyme scheme of ABA
- the first and third lines of the first stanza repeat in the following stanzas at the end alternately
- the villanelle concludes with a four-line stanza with the pattern ABAA

Guess the poetry form

Can you guess which poem was written using which form?

1. A Promise to Myself
2. A Quest for the Truth
3. A Season of both Night and Day
4. A Simple Walk…in times of Covid
5. Can't…
6. Conflicts
7. Danube Island
8. Dark Clouds
9. Different yet the Same
10. Dolphin
11. Earth's Warning
12. Every Woman's Song
13. From a portrait's view
14. Heartbreak
15. I carry you within me
16. I shall miss, when lockdown ends
17. In Shadows Cast
18. Just be
19. Labyrinth of Existence
20. Letting go of Regrets
21. No Country of my own
22. Oh, my dear world

23. Rain
24. Recipe for world war
25. Refuge within
26. State of Struggle
27. Stood Up
28. Strange Visitor
29. The Beauty of the Human Mind
30. The Pursuit of Tranquillity
31. This, too, shall pass…
32. Through Simba's eyes
33. Time for me…amid Pandemic
34. Time gone by…
35. Winter Magic
36. World

The Poems and their forms

*This list of all poems and
the form used to construct them*

1. A Promise to Myself ~ **Magic 9 poem**
2. A Quest for the Truth ~ **ABB Rhymed Poem**
3. A Season of both Night and Day ~ **Villanella Poem**
4. A Simple Walk...in times of Covid ~ **Haiku Poem**
5. Can't... ~ **Trecet Poem**
6. Conflicts ~ **Couplets Poem**
7. Danube Island ~ **Pathya Vat Poem**
8. Dark Clouds ~ **Shape Poem**
9. Different yet the Same ~ **AABB Rhymed Poem**
10. Dolphin ~ **Kennings Poem**
11. Earth's Warning ~ **Shape Poem**
12. Every Woman's Song ~ **ABCB Rhymed Poem**
13. From a portrait's view ~ **ABCB Rhymed Poem**
14. Heartbreak ~ **Landay Poem**
15. I carry you within me ~ **AABB Rhymed Poem**
16. I shall miss, when lockdown ends ~ **ABAB Rhymed Poem**
17. In Shadows Cast ~ **Villanella Poem**
18. Just be ~ **Terza Rima Poem**
19. Labyrinth of Existence ~ **Shape Poem**
20. Letting go of Regrets ~ **Terza Rima Poem**
21. No Country of my own ~ **AABB Rhymed Poem**
22. Oh, my dear world ~ **ABAB Rhymed Poem**

23. Rain ~ **ABCB Rhymed Poem**
24. Recipe for world war ~ **Free Verse Poem**
25. Refuge within ~ **Triolet Poem**
26. State of Struggle ~ **Landay Poem**
27. Stood Up ~ **Dodoitsu Poem**
28. Strange Visitor ~ **Shape Poem**
29. The Beauty of the Human Mind ~ **AABB Rhymed Poem**
30. The Pursuit of Tranquillity ~ **Villanella Poem**
31. This, too, shall pass… ~ **AABB Rhymed Poem**
32. Through Simba's eyes ~ **ABCB Rhymed Poem**
33. Time for me…amid Pandemic ~ **Free Verse Poem**
34. Time gone by… ~ **Free Verse Poem**
35. Winter Magic ~ **Magic 9 Poem**
36. World ~ **Blank Verse Poem**

About the Author

Palak Tewary

An Indian-born Londoner, is a management and finance professional, who along with being an ardent writer, is a travel buff and a photography and videography enthusiast.

She writes on travel, books, photography, business and motivation as well as poetry and fiction. She is inspired from everyday life and her work leans towards trying to provide positivity, happiness and encouragement or to inspire thoughtful consideration on social issues and self-development.

She blogs at **www.palaktewary.com** which also features her fiction, non-fiction and poetry work – including that published on various platforms.

Connect with her on:
YouTube / Twitter/X / Instagram: **@palaktewary**

Visit her **amazon page**